W9-BPK-737

A Teaspoon of Courage
for Kids

Other Books by Bradley Trevor Greive

*The Blue Day Book**

The Blue Day Journal and Directory

*Dear Mom**

Looking for Mr. Right

The Meaning of Life

The Incredible Truth About Mothers

Tomorrow

Priceless: The Vanishing Beauty of a Fragile Planet

The Book for People Who Do Too Much

*Friends to the End**

Dear Dad

The Simple Truth About Love

A Teaspoon of Courage

Dieting Causes Brain Damage

Every Day Is Christmas

For Children

The Blue Day Book for Kids

Friends to the End for Kids

*Available in Spanish

A Teaspoon of Courage for Kids

A Little Book of Encouragement for Whenever You Need It

BRADLEY TREVOR GREIVE

Andrews McMeel
Publishing, LLC
Kansas City

07 08 09 10 11 WKT 10 9 8 7 6 5 4 3 2 1

ISBN-13: 978-0-7407-6949-8
ISBN-10: 0-7407-6949-9

Library of Congress Control Number: 2007927916

www.andrewsmcmeel.com

Book design by Holly Camerlinck

ATTENTION: SCHOOLS AND BUSINESSES

Andrews McMeel books are available at quantity discounts with bulk purchase for educational, business, or sales promotional use. For information, please write to: Special Sales Department, Andrews McMeel Publishing, LLC, 4520 Main Street, Kansas City, Missouri 64111.

PHOTO CREDITS

Aflo Co. Ltd. (Japan) • www.aflo.com/en
Alamy Images (UK) • www.alamy.com
Auscape International (Australia) • www.auscape.com.au
Corbis Australia Pty Ltd. • www.corbis.com
Emerald City Images (Australia) • www.emeraldcityimages.com.au
First Light (Canada) • www.firstlight.com
Getty Images (Australia) • www.gettyimages.com
Masterfile (USA) • www.masterfile.com
Mirrorpix (UK) • www.mirrorpix.com
Photolibrary.com (Australia) • www.photolibrary.com
Ron Kimball Studios (USA) • www.ronkimballstock.com

Detailed page credits for the remarkable photographers whose work appears in *A Teaspoon of Courage for Kids* and other books by Bradley Trevor Greive are freely available at www.btgstudios.com

Sooner or later, everyone runs smack up
against a big brick wall.

Don't panic—it happens to all of us.
It doesn't matter how big or smart you are.
Life has a way of tripping us up sometimes
so things don't turn out the way we want.

Suddenly, you're stuck!
And you don't know how to get yourself
out of the mess you're in.

Maybe you're faced
with an unexpected change.

Perhaps someone around you
is suddenly acting really weird,

or maybe they're mad at you
for no good reason,

and you can't figure out what's going on.

Your first few days at a new school
can be pretty scary.

So can moving to a new town,

 going to see the doctor or the dentist,

or even when Mom brings home
a new baby brother or sister.

When you try something for the very
first time—whether it's snowboarding
or sushi—it's always a little frightening.

And it doesn't have to be a new challenge to seem so scary that we want to stay in bed all day. It can be an old problem, too.

Like shyness,

mean bullies,

or even the feeling that you're just different from everybody else, and you don't fit in.

When you're faced with troubles like these,
there's one thing you really need.

(And, no, I don't mean your favorite hideout!)

What you need is courage.

Courage is kind of like a secret weapon
you can use to defeat your foes—
and your fears.

Courage means being strong,
but you don't need big muscles,

 because courage is strength
of the heart or spirit.

It's what gives us the confidence
to do our own thing and not
just go along with the crowd.

And courage makes it possible for
little guys to stand up to big guys,
like David stood up to Goliath.

Courage doesn't mean that you're
never afraid or upset.
Even Superman cries sometimes.

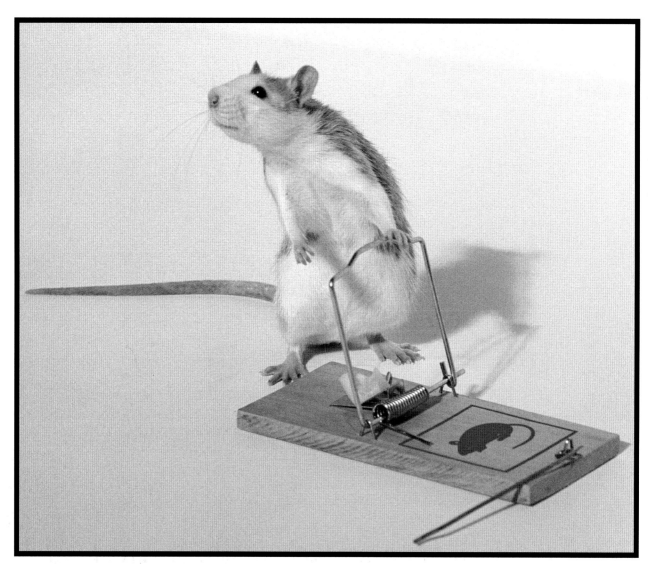

Courage means that you can
keep going and do what you need to do
even when you are scared.

In fact, fear is completely normal—
and sometimes it's very smart
to be afraid.

After all, swimming with hungry sharks
doesn't show a lot of bravery—
just a lack of brains.

So, how can *I* get a little
of this courage, you ask?

Well, that's the best part. Courage is not something you need to buy at the drugstore or the supermarket,

because you already have as much
as you could ever want inside of you!

No kidding. Whether you know it or not,
you were born with this secret weapon.

All you have to do is find it
inside yourself and let it out.

It doesn't matter how small you are—
inside every little mouse is a
courageous lion waiting to *ROAR!*

There's no denying it—the world can be a scary place sometimes.

 But instead of running away or hiding, all you have to do is stand on your own two feet (don't worry if your knees shake a little—that's normal),

then stare your fears straight in the face

and announce at full blast, "You don't scare me because I am bigger than my fears!"

"My heart is strong,
and my mind is my own!"

If you can say those words and really mean it,
an amazing new world will open up for you.

You'll soon discover that the
very things that were most scary
are really no big deal after all.

True courage can help you
overcome anything, go anywhere,
and be whatever you want.

Nothing can stand in your way now.

So what are you waiting for?
Go get 'em, Lionheart!